BOHO
CHIC

15 KNITTED
GARMENTS & ACCESSORIES

by
emily platt

QUAIL

Follow Emily at:
www.lostinknit.org
Twitter: @lostinknit

Follow Quail Publishing at:
www.quailpublishing.co.uk
Twitter: @QuailBooks
Instagram: @quailpublishing

BOHO CHIC

First published in Great Britain in 2015 by
Quail Publishing Limited
www.quailpublishing.co.uk

Designs: Emily Platt
Pattern Checking & Technical Editing: Kate Heppell
Photography: Jesse Wild
Styling: Georgina Brant for Quail Studio
Hair Design: Sharon Walker
Makeup Artist: Holly Middleton
Graphic Design: Quail Studio

ISBN 978-0-9927707-8-5

Printed in the United Kingdom

BOHO
CHIC

BOHO CHIC is a collection of hand knits for all levels of knitter, so you can create your own 'on trend' knitwear to wear camping at a festival, on holiday or just relaxing on the weekend.

With a relaxed bohemian feel, the collection is perfect for the season's trends, adding to your essential wardrobe.

Maia

cardigan

pg.76

Avia

cardigan
pg.72

Esme
cropped sweater
pg.68

Aria
slouchy hat
pg.66

Aria
pom pom
arm warmers
pg.64

Aria
blanket
pg.62

Zara
cropped cable
sweater
pg.58

Willow
textured cushion
pg.56

Primrose

slouchy hat
pg.48

Primrose

welly toppers
pg.52

Primrose

snood
pg.54

Baie
striped oversized
sweater
pg.44

Brynn
striped scarf
pg.42

Bella

looped
cardigan
pg.38

Lacey

throw/poncho

pg.34

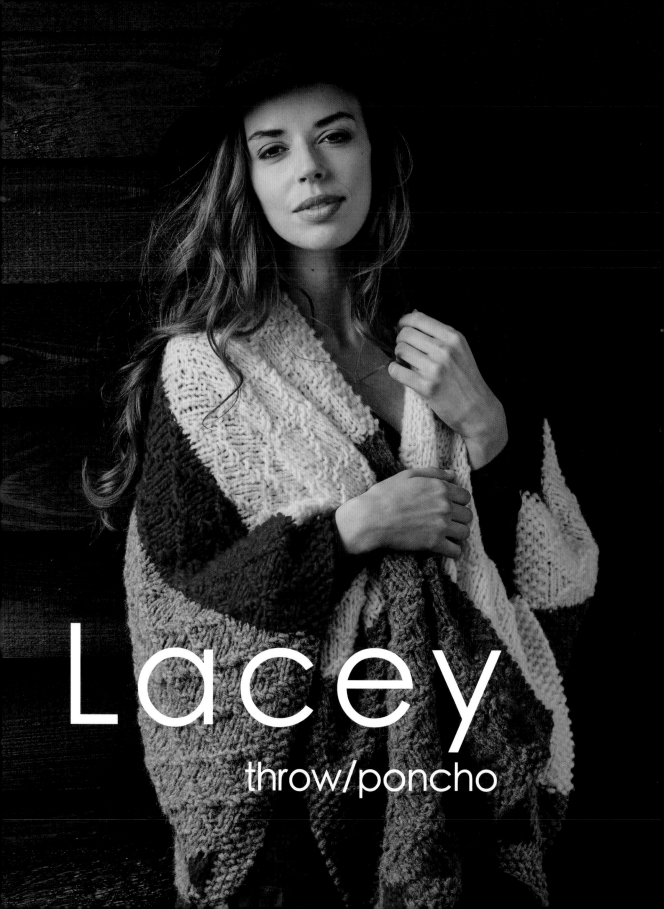

Lacey
throw/poncho

FINISHED SIZE
Each side: 100cm x 54cm

YARN
Rowan Brushed Fleece
A Crag 253   2 x 50g
B Nook 260   2 x 50g
C Cove 251   2 x 50g
D Tarn 254   3 x 50g

NEEDLES
1 pair 8mm (no 0) (US11) needles

TENSION
11 sts and 18 rows to 10cm measured over patt using 8mm (US11) needles

OTHER SUPPLIES
Tapestry needle

PATTERN INSTRUCTIONS
SIDE 1
Using 8mm (US11) needles and Yarn A, cast on 57 sts.

Work in moss st for 4 rows.

Row 1: Work in moss st for 4 sts, work row 1 of Chart A using A as MC and B as CC until 4 sts remain, moss st 4.

Continue to work chart keeping the 4 moss st correct throughout the panel.

Row 8: Work in moss st for 4 sts, P to last 4 sts, moss st 4.

Row 9 and 10: Work in moss st.

Row 11: P1, *K7, P1, rep from * to end.

Row 12: K2, P5 *K3, P5, rep from * to end.

Row 13: K1, *P2, K3, P2, K1, rep from * to end.

Row 14: P2, K2, P1, K2, *P3, K2, P1, K2, rep from * to last 2 sts, K2.

Row 15: K3, P3 *K5, P3, rep from * to last 3 sts, K3.

Row 16: P4, K1, *P7, K1* rep from * to last 4 sts, K4.

Row 17: As Row 15.

Row 18: As Row 14.

Row 19: As Row 13.

Row 20: As Row 12.

Repeat rows 11-20 three more times.

Change to Yarn B and work Rows 11-20 twice.

Change to Yarn C and work Rows 11-20 four times.

Change to Yarn D and work Rows 11-20 five times.

Next 2 Rows: Work 2 rows in moss st.

Next Row: Moss st 4, K to last 4 sts, moss st 4.

Next Row: Moss st 4, P to last 4 sts, moss st 4.

Repeat Rows 1-7.

Work in moss st for 4 rows.

Cast off all sts.

SIDE 2

Using 8mm (US11) needles and Yarn D, cast on 57 sts.

Work in moss st for 4 rows.

Row 1: Work in moss st for 4 sts, work row 1 of Chart A until 4 sts remain, moss st 4. Continue to work chart keeping the 4 moss st correct throughout the panel.

Row 8: Moss st 4, P to last 4 sts, moss st 4.

Row 9 and 10: Work in moss st.

Row 11: P1, *K7, P1, rep from * to end.

Row 12: K2, P5 *K3, P5, rep from * to end.

Row 13: K1, *P2, K3, P2, K1, rep from * to end.

Row 14: P2, K2, P1, K2, *P3, K2, P1, K2, rep from * to last 2 sts, K2.

Row 15: K3, P3 *K5, P3, rep from * to last 3 sts, K3.

Row 16: P4, K1, *P7, K1, rep from * to last 4 sts, K4.

Row 17: As Row 15.

Row 18: As Row 14.

Row 19: As Row 13.

Row 20: As Row 12.

Repeat Rows 11-20 twice more.

Change to Yarn C, repeat Rows 11-20 twice.

Change to Yarn B, repeat Rows 11-20 four times.

Change to Yarn C, repeat Rows 11-20 four times.

Change to Yarn A, repeat Rows 11-20 twice.

Next Row: Work 2 rows in moss st.

Next Row: Moss st 4, K to last 4 sts, moss st 4.

Next Row: moss st 4, P to last 4 sts, moss st 4.

Repeat Rows 1-8.

Work in moss st for 4 rows.

Cast off all sts.

MAKING UP

Place both panels next to each other and using mattress stitch sew from cast off edge until 50cm (19⅝in) have been sewn together. Sew in all ends.

Chart A

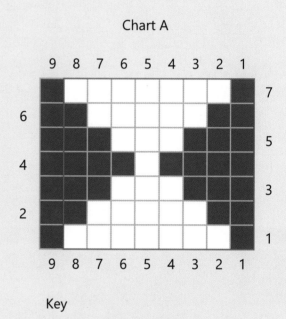

Key

MC

CC

Repeat

Bella

looped cardigan

SIZES
S [M: L: XL: XXL]

Shown in size S.
See schematic for finished measurements.
For fit information, see p.80.

YARN
Rowan Brushed Fleece
Cove 251 5 [6 : 7 : 8 : 8]   x 50g

NEEDLES
1 pair 12mm (US17) needles

TENSION
10 sts and 7 rows to 10cm measured
over stocking st using 12mm
(US17) needles

10 sts and 9 rows to 10cm over
Lace Patt using 12mm (US17) needles

8 sts and 12 rows over loop st using
12mm (US17) needles

OTHER SUPPLIES
Stitch holder
Tapestry needle

SPECIAL ABBREVIATIONS
ML: Make Loop. Knit the first stitch, but
don't take it off the needle. Hold the
yarn over your index finger and wrap the
yarn around your middle finger, forming
a loop around the middle finger. Then
knit the same stitch again and take
off the needle. You will now have two
stitches instead of one with a loop in the
middle. With the new stitches on your
right needle, take the furthest right stitch
and pull it over the stitch to the left and
off the needle. Now there is only one
stitch again and the loop is secured.

PATTERN INSTRUCTIONS
BACK
Using 12mm (US17) needles, cast on
44 [48: 54: 60: 64] sts.

Rows 1-6: Work in 2x2 rib.
Work in st st for 14 rows.
Next Row: K1, *yfwd, k2tog, rep from
* to last st, K1.
Next Row: Purl.
Next Row: K2, *yfwd, k2tog, rep from
* to end*.
Next Row: Purl.
Rep these last 4 rows (which form Lace
Pattern) for 20 rows.
Work in st st for 22 rows.
Work in Lace Pattern for 20 rows.
Work in st st for 10 rows, finishing after a
WS row.

ARMHOLE SHAPING
Next Row: Cast off 3 sts, K to end.
41 [45: 51: 57: 61] sts.
Next Row: Cast off 3 sts, P to end.
38 [42: 48: 54: 58] sts.
Next Row: K2tog, K to last 2 sts, k2tog.
36 [40: 46: 52: 56] sts.

Next Row: P2tog, P to last 2 sts, p2tog. 34 [38: 44: 50: 54] sts.
Next Row: K2tog, ML to last 2 sts, k2tog. 32 [36: 42: 48: 52] sts.
Next Row: Purl.
Next Row: K2tog, ML to last 2 sts, k2tog. 30 [34: 40: 46: 50] sts.
Next Row: Purl.
Next Row: K1, ML to last st, K1.
Next Row: Purl.
Rep these last 2 rows 6 [6: 7: 8: 8] times more.

SHAPE BACK NECK
Next Row (RS): K1, (ML) 6 [6: 8: 10: 10] times, k2tog, turn leaving rem 21 [25: 29: 33: 37] stitches on a holder. 8 [8: 10: 12: 12] sts.
Next Row: P2tog, P to end. 7 [7: 9: 11: 11] sts.
Next Row: K1, ML to last st, K1.
Next Row: P2tog, P to end. 6 [6: 8: 10: 10] sts.
Cast off.
Place sts from holder back onto needle, ready to work a RS row. With RS facing, rejoin yarn at the RH edge of the work.
Next Row: Cast off 12 [16: 18: 20: 24] sts, ssk, (ML) 6 [6: 8: 10: 10] times, k1. 8 [8: 10: 12: 12] sts.
Next Row: P to last 2 sts, p2tog. 7 [7: 9: 11: 11] sts.
Next Row: K1, ML to last st, K1.
Next Row: P to last 2 sts, p2tog. 6 [6: 8: 10: 10] sts.
Cast off.

LEFT FRONT
***Using 12mm (US17) needles, cast on 24 [24: 28: 30: 30] sts.

Rows 1-6: Work in 2x2 rib.
Row 7: K to last 3 sts, P1, K1, P1.

Row 8 and all WS rows to 112 [112, 114, 116, 116]: P1, K1, P to end.
Rows 9-16: Rep rows 7-8 four more times.
Row 17: *K1, ML to last 3 sts, P1, K1, P1.
Rows 19-20: As rows 17-18.
Row 21: *K1, *yfwd, k2tog,* rep from * to last 3 sts, P1, K1, P1.
Row 23: *K2, *yfwd, k2tog,* rep from * to last 4 sts, (K1, P1) twice.
Rows 25-40: As rows 21-24.
Rows 41-58: As rows 7-8.
Rows 59-62: As rows 17-20.
Rows 63-82: As rows 21-40.
Rows 83-92: As rows 7-8.***

UNDERARM AND FRONT SHAPING
Row 93: Cast off 3 [3: 4: 3: 3] sts, K to last 3 sts, P1, K1, P1. 21 [21: 24: 27: 27] sts.
Row 95: K2tog, K to last 3 sts, P1, K1, P1. 20 [20: 23: 26: 26] sts.
Row 97: K2tog, ML to last 3 sts, P1, K1, P1. 19 [19: 22: 25: 25] sts.
Row 99: K1, ML to last 3 sts, p1, k1, p1.
Row 101: K2tog, ML to last 3 sts, P1, K1, P1. 18 [18: 21: 24: 24] sts.
Row 103: K1, ML to last 4 sts, p2tog, K1, P1. 17 [17: 20: 23: 23] sts.
Rows 105, 107, 109 & 111: As row 103. 16 [16: 19: 22: 22] sts.

SIZES L, XL AND XXL ONLY:
Next Row: As row 103. - [-: 15: 18: 18] sts.

SIZES XL AND XXL ONLY:
Next Row: As row 103. - [-: -: 17: 17] sts.

ALL SIZES: Next WS Row: P1, K1, p2tog, P to end. 12 [12: 14: 16: 16] sts.

Rep the last 2 rows three more times. 6 [6: 8: 10: 10] sts.
Cast off.

RIGHT FRONT

Work as for left side, reversing all shaping

MAKING UP

Using mattress stitch and with RS facing,
sew up the shoulder seams.
Pin the sides together and leave a gap of
15cm for the side split at the bottom.
Sew up using mattress stitch.

SCHEMATIC

Shows finished measurements

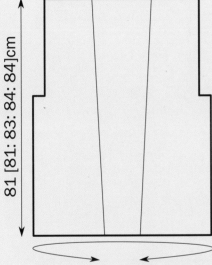

81 [81: 83: 84: 84]cm

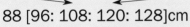

88 [96: 108: 120: 128]cm

Brynn
striped scarf

FINISHED SIZE
45cm x 170cm

YARN
Rowan Brushed Fleece
A Tarn 254   5 x 100g
B Cove 251   1 x 100g

NEEDLES
1 pair 15mm (US19) needles

TENSION
5 sts and 7 rows to 10cm measured over pattern on 15mm (US19) needles

OTHER SUPPLIES
Crochet hook or latchook

PATTERN INSTRUCTIONS
Using 15mm (US19) needles and 2 strands of Yarn A held together, cast on 23sts
Knit 4 rows.
Begin working in the following pattern;
Row 1: K3, *sl 1 purlwise, K3, rep from * to end.
Row 2: K3, *sl 1 purlwise wyif, K3, repeat from * to end.
Row 3: K1, *sl 1 purlwise wyif, K3, repeat from * to last 2 sts, sl 1 purlwise wyif, K1.
Row 4: P1, sl 1 purlwise wyif, *P3, sl 1 purlwise wyif, repeat from *to last st, P1.
Repeat these 4 rows 3 times more.
**Change to 1 strand of Yarn A and 1 strand of Yarn B and work 3 repeats.
Change to 2 strands of Yarn A and work 5 repeats**
Repeat from ** to ** 6 times more.
Change to 1 strand of Yarn A and 1 strand of Yarn B and work 3 repeats.
Change to 2 strands of Yarn A and work 4 repeats.
Knit 4 rows.
Cast off.

TASSELS
Cut out 30cm long lengths of Yarn A. Using a crochet hook or latchhook, fold two lengths of Yarn A together and attach along cast on and cast off edges.

Baie
striped oversized sweater

SIZES

XS/S [M/L: XL/2X]
Shown in size M/L

See schematic for finished measurements.
For fit information, see p.80.

YARN

Rowan Cocoon
A Duck Down 833   4 [4: 5] x 50g

Rowan Fazed Tweed
B Yew 004   4 [4: 5] x 50g

Rowan Silkystones
C Tarn 087   2 [2:3] x 50g

NEEDLES

1 pair 7mm (no2) needles

TENSION

13 sts x 15 rows to 10cm measured
over pattern

PATTERN INSTRUCTIONS
BACK

Using 7mm needles and yarn A cast on
81 [91: 101] sts.

Work in 1x1 rib for 8 rows.

Next 2 rows: Knit
Row 1: Using yarn B, K1 *yfwd, k2tog, rep
from * to end.
Row 2: Purl.
Row 3: *K2tog, yfwd, rep from * to last st, K1.
Row 4: Purl.
Row 5: Knit.
Row 6: Purl.
Rows 7-10: Change to Yarn A, knit.
Rows 11, 13 & 15: Change to Yarn C, knit.
Rows 12, 14 & 16: Purl.
Row 17: Change to Yarn A, knit.
Row 18: Purl
Row 19: *K1, yfwd, rep from * to last st, K1.
Row 20: *P1, drop yfwd st* to last st, P1.
Row 21: Change to Yarn B, Knit.
Row 22: Purl.
Row 23: K1 *yfwd, k2tog, rep from *
to end.
Row 24: Purl
Row 25: *K2tog, yfwd, rep from * to last st, K1.
Row 27: Knit.
Row 28: Purl.
Row 29 (RS): Change to Yarn A, purl.
Row 30: Knit
Row 31: Purl.
Row 32: Knit,
Row 33: Change to Yarn C, knit.
Row 34: Purl.
Row 35: *K1, yfwd, rep from * to last st, K1.
Row 36: *P1, drop yfwd st* to last st, P1.
Row 37: Change to Yarn A, knit.
Row 38: Purl.

These 38 rows complete the
repeat pattern.
Rep Rows 1-38 once more, then work Rows
1-10 once.
Next Row: Keeping the pattern correct,
work 30 [35: 40] sts and turn leaving the
remaining sts on a holder
Next Row (WS): Work even in patt.
Next Row: Work until 2 sts remain, k2tog.
Next Row: K2tog, work to end.
Next Row: Work until 2 sts remain, k2tog.
Next Row: Work even in patt.
Cast off rem sts.
With RS facing rejoin yarn and cast off
centre sts.
Work other side of neck reversing
all shaping.

FRONT

Work as for back until 88 rows have
been worked.

Work 34 [39: 44] sts and turn leaving
remaining sts on a holder.
Keeping pattern correct, k2tog at beg of
the next 3 rows
Next Row (WS): Work in patt.
Next Row: K2tog, work in patt to end.
Repeat these 2 rows 3 more times.
Work 2 rows in patt.
Cast off rem.
With RS facing, rejoin yarn and cast
off centre.
Work the other side of neck reversing
all shaping.

SLEEVES (MAKE 2)

Using Yarn A and 7mm needles, cast on
63 [69: 75] sts.

Work in 1x1 rib for 6 rows
Row 1: Knit.
Row 2: Purl.
Work in pattern as for body until 44 rows
have been worked.
Cast off.

SEWING UP

With right sides facing, sew together both
shoulder seams using mattress stitch.

NECK TRIM

Using 7mm circular needles and Yarn A
pick up 12 sts down left neck, 9 sts across
front, 12 sts up right neck, 7 sts down side
neck, 19sts across back, 7 sts up back neck.
66 sts.
Work in 1x1 rib for 6 rnds.
Cast off stitches loosely.
Attach sleeves and side seams using
mattress stitch.
Sew in all ends.

SCHEMATIC
Shows finished measurements

FRONT/BACK

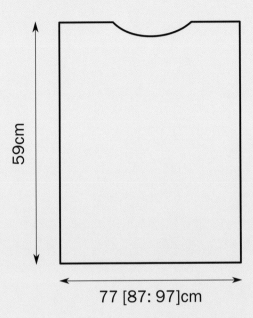

59cm

77 [87: 97]cm

SLEEVES

60 [66: 71]cm

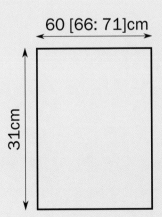

31cm

Primrose

slouchy hat

SIZE
56cm (22in) circumference
30cm (12in) height without bobble

YARN
Rowan Brushed Fleece
Grotto 257   1 x 100g

NEEDLES
1 pair 8mm (no 0) (US 11) needles

TENSION
15 sts and 14 rows to 10cm measured over
bobble patt using 8mm
(US 11) needles

OTHER SUPPLIES
Tapestry needle

PATTERN INSTRUCTIONS
BRIM

Using 8mm (US11) needles, cast on
75 sts.

Row 1: *K1, P1, rep from * to last st, K1.
Row 2: *P1, K1, rep from * to last st, P1.
Rep Rows 1-2 six more times, then Row 1
once.
Row 16: *P1, K1, rep from * to last 3 sts,
P1, K2tog. 74 sts.

BODY
Row 1(RS): Purl
Row 2: K1, *(K1, P1, K1) into the next st,
P3tog, rep from * to last st, K1.
Row 3: Purl
Row 4: K1, *P3tog, (K1, P1, K1) into next
st, rep from * to last st, K1.
Rows 1-4 form Bobble pattern. Rep Rows
1-4 twice more.

CROWN DECREASES
Next Row: P1, [P7, p2tog] 8 times, P1.
66 sts.
Work Rows 2-4 of Bramble pattern.
Next Row: P1, [P6, p2tog] 8 times, P1.
58 sts.
Work Rows 2-4 of Bramble pattern.
Next Row: P1, [P5, p2tog] 8 times, P1.
50 sts.
Work Rows 2-4 of Bramble pattern.
Next Row: P1, [P4, p2tog] 8 times, P1.
42 sts.
Work Rows 2-4 of Bramble pattern.
Next Row: P1, [P3, p2tog] 8 times, P1.
34 sts.
Work Row 2 of Bramble pattern.
Next Row: P1, [P2, p2tog] 8 times, P1.
26 sts.
Next Row: P1, [P1, p2tog] 8 times, P1.
18 sts.

Break yarn, thread onto darning needle,
pull through rem sts and pull tight
to fasten.

With RS together sew seam together using
mattress st. Using remaining yarn, create a
pom pom 12cm (5in) in diameter. Sew on
the top of the hat, making sure it is secure.

Primrose

welly toppers

SIZE
23cm tall
32cm circumference

YARN
Rowan Brushed Fleece
Grotto 257   2 x 100g

NEEDLES
1 pair 8mm (no 0) (US 11) needles

TENSION
14 sts and 14 rows to 10cm measured over patt using 8mm (US 11) needles

ABBREVIATIONS
C4B: Cable 4 back. Slip to sts to Cable Needle, hold in back. K2 from LH needle, K2 from Cable Needle.

C4F: Cable 4 front. Slip to sts to Cable Needle, hold in front. K2 from LH needle, K2 from Cable Needle.

OTHER SUPPLIES
Tapestry needle
Cable needle

PATTERN INSTRUCTIONS
WELLY TOPPER (MAKE 2)

Using 8mm (US 11) needles, cast on 32 sts.

Row 1: (K1, P1) twice, P2, K4, P2, K8, P2, K4, P2, (K1, P1) twice.
Row 2 and all even rows: (K1, P1) twice, K2, P4, K2, P8, K2, P4, K2, (K1, P1) twice.
Row 3 and 5: As Row 1.
Row 7: (K1, P1) twice, P2, C4F, P2, C4B, C4F, P2, C4F, P2, (K1, P1) twice.
Continue working these 8 rows until work measures 32cm (12½in).
Cast off.

MAKING UP
With cast on and cast off edge together, using mattress st sew together.
Sew in all ends.
Make 4 pompoms measuring 4.5mm (1¾in) in diameter.
Cut 2 lengths of yarn measuring 50cm (19⅝in).
Thread the yarn through the top of the welly topper in between the moss stitch and first cable. On each end thread a pompom and secure. Repeat for the second welly topper.

Primrose

snood

SIZE
100cm (40in) circumference
42cm (16in) height

YARN
Rowan Brushed Fleece
Grotto 257   4x 100g

NEEDLES
1 pair 8mm (no 0) (US 11) needles

TENSION
15 sts and 14 rows to 10cm measured over
bobble patt using 8mm (US 11) needles

OTHER SUPPLIES
Tapestry needle

PATTERN INSTRUCTIONS
Using 8mm (US11) needles, cast on
62 sts.

Row 1 (RS): Purl
Row 2: K1, *(K1, P1, K1) into the next st,
p3tog*, rep from * to last st, K1.
Row 3: Purl.
Row 4: K1, *P3tog, (K1, P1, K1) into next
st, rep from * to last st, K1
Rep Rows 1-4 until work measures 103cm.
Cast off.

MAKING UP
With Cast on and Cast off edge touching,
use mattress st to sew up.
Sew in all ends.

Willow

textured cushion

SIZE
60cm square

YARN
Rowan Big Wool Colour
Carnival 103   5 x 100g

NEEDLES
1 pair 12mm (US17) needles

TENSION
7 sts and 12 rows to 10cm measured over
stocking st using 12mm
(US17) needles

8 sts and 10 rows to 10cm measured over
pattern using 12mm (US17) needles

OTHER SUPPLIES
Tapestry needle

PATTERN INSTRUCTIONS
FRONT

Using 12mm (US17) needles, cast on
50 sts.

Row 1: Purl.
Row 2: Knit.
Row 3: Purl.
Row 4: K1, *P3, slip 2 purlwise with yarn at
front, P3, rep from * to last st, K1.
Row 5: K1, *K3, slip 2 purlwise with yarn at
back, K3, rep from * to last st, K1.
Repeat rows 4-5 twice more.
Row 10: K1, *P3, slip 2 purlwise, P3, rep
from * to last st, k1.
Repeat rows 1-10 until work measures
52cm (20½in).
Cast off knitwise.

BACK (make 2)
Using 12mm (US17) needles, cast on
43 sts.
Work in 1x1 rib for 3 rows
Continue in stocking stitch for 32cm
starting with a purl row
Cast off knitwise.

MAKE UP
With RS facing lay the back panels over the
front panel with an overlap in the middle.
Pin the cushion together and sew around
the edge using mattress stitch.
Sew in all ends

Zara
cropped cable
sweater

SIZES
XS [S: M: L: XL: XXL]

Shown in size XS
See schematic for finished measurements.
For fit information, see p.80.

YARN
Rowan Super Fine Merino DK
Marble 143   8 [10: 10: 11: 13: 15] x 50g

Photographed in Marble (143)

NEEDLES
1 pair 5mm (no6 (US8) needles

TENSION
18 sts and 28 rows to 10cm measured over
Cable and Mesh pattern.

20 sts and 28 rows to 10cm measured
over Moss st.

PATTERN INSTRUCTIONS
BACK

Using 5mm (US8) needles cast on
88 [98: 102: 118: 128: 136] sts.

Work in Moss st for 6 rows
Knit 1 row and evenly decrease
8 [10: 10: 10: 12: 12] sts along row.
80 [88: 92: 108: 116: 124] sts.
Purl 1 row.
Begin working in Cable and Mesh pattern
with Moss edges as follows:

Row 1: Moss st 10 [10: 12: 12: 16: 16],
work 3 [4: 4: 6: 6: 7] reps of Mesh patt,
work Cable A, work 3 [4: 4: 6: 6: 7] reps of
Mesh patt, work Cable B, work
3 [4: 4: 6: 6: 7] reps of Mesh patt, work
Cable C, work 3 [4: 4: 6: 6: 7] reps of Mesh
patt, Moss st 10 [10: 12: 12: 16: 16] sts. You
may find it useful to place a stitch marker
between each pattern section at this point.
Row 2: Moss st 10 [10: 12: 12: 16: 16],
P6 [8: 8: 12: 12: 14], work Cable C,
P6 [8: 8: 12: 12: 14], work Cable B,
P6 [8: 8: 12: 12: 14], work Cable A,
P6 [8: 8: 12: 12: 14], Moss st
10 [10: 12: 12: 16: 16] sts.
These rows establish patt. Cont working
in patt until work measures 25cm/10in
from cast-on edge, finishing after a WS
row. Make a note of which pattern row you
finished on, so that you can match your
front and back.

ARMHOLE SHAPING

Cont working in pattern, keeping stitches correct.

Cast off 4 [4: 4: 4: 5: 5] sts at beg of next 2 rows. 72 [80: 84: 100: 106: 114] sts.

Dec 1 st at each end of next 4 [4: 4: 5: 5: 7] rows. 64 [72: 76: 90: 96: 100] sts.

Dec 1 st at each end of next 2 [2: 2: 3: 4: 2] alt rows. 60 [68: 72: 84: 88: 96] sts.

**

Cont working straight without further shaping, keeping pattern correct, on the rem 60 [68: 72: 84: 88: 96] sts for 40 [42: 48: 48: 50: 54] rows.

SHOULDER SHAPING

Cast off 6 [7: 7: 8: 9: 10] sts at beg of next 6 rows.

Leave rem 24 [26: 30: 36: 34: 36] sts on holder.

FRONT

Work as for back to **.

Cont working straight without further shaping, keeping pattern correct, on the rem 60 [68: 72: 84: 88: 96] sts for 24 [26: 32: 32: 34: 38] rows, finishing after a WS row.

NECK AND SHOULDERS

Next Row (RS): Work 23 [26: 26: 29: 32: 35] sts in patt. Place marker – this is the neck edge. Turn.

Next Row (WS): P2tog, work in patt to end. 1 st dec'd.

Next Row: Work in patt to marker. Turn. Rep these last 2 rows 4 times more.

Next Row: Cast off 6 [7: 7: 8: 9: 10] sts, work in patt to marker. Turn.

Next Row: Work in patt.
Rep the last 2 rows twice more.
All shoulder sts cast off.

Place centre 14 [16: 20: 26: 24: 26] sts on holder.

Rejoin yarn to work other shoulder, starting with a RS row.

Next Row (RS): K2tog, work in patt to end. 1 st dec'd.

Next Row: Work in patt to end.
Rep these last 2 rows 4 times more.

Next Row: Cast off 6 [7: 7: 8: 9: 10] sts, work in patt to end.

Next Row: Work in patt.
Rep the last 2 rows twice more.
All shoulder sts cast off.

SLEEVES (MAKE 2)

Cast on 54 [58: 62: 66: 74: 82] sts.
Work 8 rows in Moss st.

Next Row: Work 10 [10: 12: 12: 16: 16] sts Moss st,
12 [14: 14: 16: 16: 22] sts mesh st, 10 sts Cable A, 12 [14: 14: 16: 16: 22] sts mesh st, 10 [10: 12: 12: 16: 16] sts Moss st.

This row establishes pattern. Work even in pattern until sleeve measures 42 [43: 43: 44.5: 44.5: 45.5]cm/ 16.5 [17: 17: 17.5: 17.5: 18]in.

Cast off 4 [4: 4: 5: 5: 5] sts at beg of next 2 rows. 46 [50: 54: 56: 64: 76] sts.

Dec 1 st at each end of next 4 [4: 4: 5: 5: 7] rows. 38 [42: 46: 46: 54: 62] sts.

Dec 1 st at each end of next 2 [2: 2: 3: 4: 2] alt rows. 34 [38: 42: 40: 46: 58] sts.

Work 18 [18: 16: 20: 16: 8] rows even in patt.

Dec 1 st at beg of next 12 [16: 20: 18: 24: 36] rows. 22 sts.

Cast off 3 sts at beg of next 4 rows.

Cast off rem 10 sts.

MAKING UP
With RS together, using mattress stitch sew up both shoulder seams.

With a 5mm circular needle, pick up 15 sts down side neck, sts from front holder, 15 sts from other side of neck and sts from back holder.

Work in moss stitch for 5 rnds.

Cast off all sts loosely.

STITCH PATTERNS
MOSS STITCH
Row 1 (RS, odd number of sts): K1, P1, rep from * to end.

Rep Row 1 for pattern.

When decreasing in Moss st, work K over P and P over K.

MESH PATTERN
Row 1 (RS): *Yfwd, k2tog, rep from * to end.

Row 2 & 4: Purl.

Row 3: *K2tog, yfwd, rep from * to end.

Rep Rows 1-4.

CABLE A
Row 1, 3, 5 & 7: P2, k6, p2.

Row 2 and all WS rows: K2, P6, K2.

Row 9: P2, C6B, P2.

Rep Rows 1-10.

CABLE B
Row 1, 3, 5 & 7: P2, k12, p2.

Row 2 and all WS rows: K2, P12, K2.

Row 9: P2, C6B, C6F, P2.

Rep Rows 1-10.

CABLE C
Row 1, 3, 5 & 7: P2, k6, p2.

Row 2 and all WS rows: K2, P6, K2.

Row 9: P2, C6F, P2.

Rep Rows 1-10.

SCHEMATIC
Shows finished measurements

FRONT/BACK

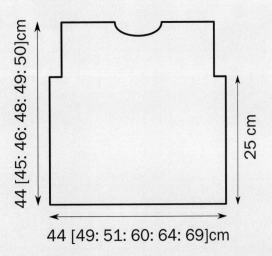

44 [45: 46: 48: 49: 50]cm

25 cm

44 [49: 51: 60: 64: 69]cm

SLEEVE

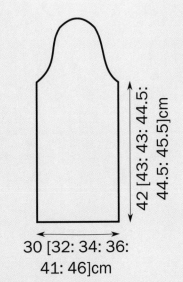

42 [43: 43: 44.5: 44.5: 45.5]cm

30 [32: 34: 36: 41: 46]cm

Aria
blanket

SIZE
80cm x 60cm

YARN
Rowan Big Wool Colour
Fairground 102   13 x 100g

NEEDLES
1 pair of 12mm (US17) needles

TENSION
7 sts and 12 rows to 10cm measured over
St st on 12mm (US17) needles

OTHER SUPPLIES
Large tapestry needle
Crochet hook or latch hook

PATTERN INSTRUCTIONS
SQUARES (MAKE 12)

Using 12mm needles cast on 25 sts.

Rows 1-3: *K1, P1, rep from * to last st, K1.
Row 4: K1, P1, K1, K to last 3 sts, K1, P1, K1.
Row 5: K1, P1, K1, P to last 3 sts, K1, P1, K1.
Rep Rows 4-5 fifteen more times.
Rep Rows 1-3 once.
Cast off.

MAKING UP
Place squares so that 1 square is placed right way up and the next square is placed at 90 degrees celsius. Continue to place the squares in this way with 3 squares in each row. This should create a chequerboard effect in the knitting.

Using mattress stitch, join up each square to produce one giant square.

TASSELS
Cut out 30cm (11¾in) long lengths of big wool colour. Using a crochet hook or latchhook, fold two lengths of Big Wool together and attach down one side of the throw. Continue down the entire side and then repeat this on the opposite side.

Aria

pom pom
arm warmers

SIZE
20cm long
25cm circumference

YARN
Rowan Big Wool Colour
Fete 101   1 x 100g

NEEDLES
1 pair 8mm (no 0) (US 11) needles

TENSION
8 sts and 12 rows to 10cm measured over
patt using 8mm (US 11) needles

OTHER SUPPLIES
Tapestry needle

PATTERN INSTRUCTIONS
ARM WARMERS (MAKE 2)

Using 8mm (US11) needles, cast on 22 sts.
Work in 2x2 rib until work measures 20cm.
Cast off loosely.

MAKING UP
With RS together and side seams lined up,
start at one end and sew up 3cm. Leave a
7cm opening and continue to sew up the
remaining side seam.

Make 4 pompoms each measuring 45mm
diameter.

With arm warmer in front of you attach first
pompom 5 cms from edge on opposite
side to thumb hole. Then position the next
pompom close to the first in line.

Repeat for the second arm warmer.

Aria
slouchy hat

SIZE
56cm circumference
30cm height

YARN
Rowan Big Wool Colour
Fairground 102   1 x 100g

NEEDLES
1 pair of 10mm (no 000) (US15) needles

TENSION
7 sts and 12 rows to 10cm measured over patt on 10mm (US15) needles

OTHER SUPPLIES
Tapestry needle

PATTERN INSTRUCTIONS
HAT

Using 10mm (US15) needles, cast on 40 sts.

Work in 1x1 rib for 6cm.

Row 1: K4, *yfwd, k2tog, K2, rep from * to end.
Row 2: Purl.
Row 3: K4, *k2tog, yfwd, K2, rep from * to end.
Row 4: Purl.
Rep Rows 1-4 until work measures 20cm.
Next Row: K4, *yfwd, k2tog, K2, rep from * to end.
Next Row: [P3, p2tog] 8 times. 32 sts
Next Row: K4, *k2tog, yfwd, K2, rep from * to end.
Next Row: [P2, p2tog] 8 times. 24 sts.
Next Row: K2tog until end. 12 sts.
Next Row: Purl.
Break yarn, thread through remaining sts and pull tight to fasten.

MAKING UP
With RS facing join side seams using mattress stitch. Make a pompom with a diameter of 100mm and sew securely into the cast off edge of the hat.

Sew in all ends.

Esme

cropped sweater

SIZES

XS [S: M: L: XL: XXL]

Shown in size XS
See schematic for finished measurements.
For fit information, see p.80.

YARN

Rowan Fazed Tweed
A Elderberry 011
7 [8: 9: 10: 11: 13] x 50g

Rowan Cocoon
B Mountain 805   1 x 50g

NEEDLES

1 pair 7mm (no2) (No US equivalent)
needles

7mm circular needle, 40cm

TENSION

14 sts and 24 rows to 10cm measured
over pattern

PATTERN INSTRUCTIONS
BACK & FRONT

Using 7mm needles and Yarn A cast on
60 [68: 72: 80: 88: 96] sts.

Rows 1-4: Work in 2x2 rib.
Row 5: Knit.
Row 6: Purl.
Row 7: Change to yarn B, knit.
Row 8: Purl.
Row 5: Change to Yarn A, knit.
Row 6: Purl.
Now work in Textured Pattern until work
measures 23 [24: 24: 25: 25: 26]cm/
9 [9.5: 9.6: 10: 10: 10.5]in.
Cast off 3 [3: 4: 5: 6: 7] sts at beg of next
2 rows. 54 [62: 64: 70: 76: 82] sts.
K2tog at each end of next 3 [3: 3: 5: 5: 7]
rows. 48 [56: 58: 60: 66: 68] sts.
K2tog at each end of next 3 [3: 4: 3: 5: 4]
alternate rows. 42 [50: 50: 54: 56: 60] sts.
Continue straight until work measures
39 [41: 43: 45: 46: 48]cm.
Next Row (RS): Work 13 [16: 16: 17: 17: 18] sts
and turn leaving remaining sts
on holder.
Next Row: P2tog, work to end.
Next Row: Cast off 5 [6: 6: 7: 7: 8] sts,
work until 2 sts remain, k2tog.
Cast off remaining 6 [8: 8: 8: 8: 8] sts.
With RS facing, rejoin yarn and cast off
centre 16 [18: 18: 20: 22: 24] sts, then k to
end. 13 [16: 16: 17: 17: 18]sts.
Work the other side of neck, reversing all
shaping as follows;
Next Row (WS): Cast off 5 [6: 6: 7: 7: 8] sts,
work until 2 sts remain, p2tog.
Next Row: K2tog, work to end.
Cast off remaining 6 [8: 8: 8: 8: 8] sts.

SLEEVES (MAKE 2)

Using 7mm needles and Yarn A cast on 38 [40: 42: 44: 50: 58] sts.

Work in Textured Stitch for 6 rows.
Next Row (RS): Change to Yarn B, knit.
Next Row: Purl.
Next Row: Change to Yarn A, knit.
Next Row: Purl.
Work 17 rows in Textured Stitch pattern.
Next Row: Kfb, work in patt to last st, kfb.
2 sts inc'd.
Rep these 18 rows 3 more times. 46 [48: 50: 52: 58: 66] sts.
Cont working straight in patt until sleeve measures 47 [48: 48: 49.5: 49.5: 50.5]cm/ 19 [19: 19: 19.5: 19.5: 20]in from cast-on edge.
Cast off 3 [3: 4: 5: 6: 7] sts at beg of the next 2 rows. 40 [42: 42: 42: 46: 52] sts
K2tog at each end of next
3 [3: 3: 5: 5: 7] rows. 34 [36: 36: 32: 36: 38] sts.
K2tog at each end of next 3 [3: 4: 3: 5: 4] alternate rows. 28 [30: 28: 26: 26: 30] sts.
Work 2 [2: 4: 8: 10: 8] rows even in patt.
Cont in patt, dec 1 st at beg of next
18 [18: 16: 12: 12: 14] rows.
Cast off rem 10 [12: 12: 14: 14: 16] sts.

MAKING UP

With RS together, join shoulder seams using mattress st.

NECK TRIM

Using 7mm circular needles, pick up sts around neckline, 14sts per 10cm, in a multiple of 4.
Work in 2x2 rib for 5 rows.
Knit 5 rows.
Cast off all sts loosely.

Using mattress st sew in sleeves and then sew together side seams.
Sew in all ends.

STITCH PATTERNS
2X2 Rib

Row 1: *K2, P2, rep from * to end.
Rep Row 1 for patt.

TEXTURED STITCH

Row 1: *K1, slip stitch purlwise with yarn in front, rep from * to last 2 sts, K2.
Row 2: Purl.
Row 3: K2, *slip stitch purlwise with yarn in front, k1, rep from * to end.
Row 4: Purl.
Rep Rows 1-4 for patt.

SCHEMATIC
Shows finished measurements

FRONT/BACK

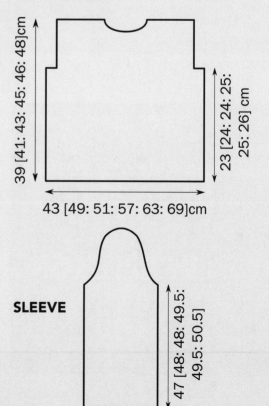

39 [41: 43: 45: 46: 48]cm

23 [24: 24: 25: 25: 26] cm

43 [49: 51: 57: 63: 69]cm

SLEEVE

47 [48: 48: 49.5: 49.5: 50.5]

Avia
cardigan

SIZES
XS [S: M: L: XL: XXL]

Shown in size XS
See schematic for finished measurements.
For fit information, see p.80.

YARN
Rowan Cocoon
A Mountain 805   5 [6: 7: 7: 8: 9] x 100g
B Polar 801   4 [5: 6: 6: 7: 7] x 100g

NEEDLES
1 pair 7mm (no 2)
(no US equivalent) needles

TENSION
14.5 sts and 18 rows to 10cm measured
over pattern on 7mm needles

PATTERN INSTRUCTIONS
BACK

Using 7mm needles and Yarn A cast on
73 [81: 91: 99: 109: 117] sts.

Row 1 (Moss st): *K1, P1, rep from * to
last st, K1.
Next row: K2 [2: 1: 1: 2: 2], *yfwd, k2tog,
K3, rep from * to last 3 [3: 2: 2: 3: 3] sts,
yfwd, k2tog, K1 [1: 0: 0: 1: 1].
Work in Moss st for 8 rows
Next Row (RS): Change to Yarn B, knit,
work m1 in middle of row for sizes
S, L, XXL. 73 [82: 91: 100: 109: 118] sts.
Next Row: Purl.
Work 0 [0: 2: 2: 4: 4] rows in St st.
Beg working colourwork patt from Chart,
working the first st once and the following
9-st rep 8 [9: 10: 11: 12: 13] times.
Work Rows 1-40 of chart once, work
0 [0: 0: 0: 2: 2] rows St st.
Work Rows 1-40 of chart once, work
0 [0: 2: 2: 4: 4] rows St st.

Neck Shaping
Next Row (RS): Cast off 8 [9: 10: 11: 12:
13) sts, K16 [18: 20: 22: 24: 26], turn.
Next Row: P2tog, purl to end. 15 [17: 19:
21: 23: 25] sts
Next Row: Cast off 8 [9: 10: 11: 12: 13] sts,
K7 [8: 9: 10: 11: 12], turn.
Next Row: P2tog, purl to end. 6 [7: 8: 9:
10: 11] sts.
Next Row: Cast off 6 [7: 8: 9: 10: 11] sts
for shoulder, place a removable stitch
marker, cast off 25 [28: 31: 34: 37: 40) sts
for centre neck, place a removable stitch
marker, k2tog, k to end.
Next Row (WS): Cast off
8 [9: 10: 11: 12: 13] sts, purl to end.
Next Row: K2tog, knit to end. 15 [17: 19:
21: 23: 25] sts.

Next Row: Cast off 8 [9: 10: 11: 12: 13] sts, knit to end.
Next Row: K2tog, knit to end.
6 [7: 8: 9: 10: 11] sts.
Cast off rem sts.

RIGHT FRONT

Using 7mm needles and Yarn A cast on 41 [43: 47: 49: 53: 55] sts
Row 1 (Moss st): *K1, P1, rep from * to last st, K1.
Next row: K2 [1: 1: 2: 2: 1], *yfwd, k2tog, K3, rep from * to last 3 [2: 2: 3: 3: 2] sts, yfwd, k2tog, K1 [0: 0: 1: 1: 0].
Work in Moss st for 8 rows
Next Row (RS): Work Moss st over first 7 sts, place marker, change to Yarn B and knit, work m1 in middle of row for sizes S, L, XXL. 41 [44: 47: 50: 53: 56] sts.
Next Row: Purl in yarn B to marker, sm, work in Moss st in Yarn A to end.

NOTE: Read this section through in full before you continue, as you will be working two sets of instructions at once.

Work 0 [0: 2: 2: 4: 4] rows in St st and Moss St as set.
Next Row: Moss st 7, work colourwork patt from chart to end. Note that you will be working incomplete repeats of the chart.
Work Rows 1-40 of chart once, work 0 [0: 0: 0: 2: 2] rows St st and Moss st.
Work Rows 1-40 of chart once, work 0 [0: 2: 2: 4: 4] rows St st and Moss st.
You may find it useful to use stitch markers to help you keep track of the colourwork pattern.

AT THE SAME TIME, dec 1 st on every 10th RS row as follows:
Moss st 7 in Yarn A, sm, k2tog in Yarn B, work in patt to end. 1 st dec'd.
After all decs have been worked,

24 [27: 30: 33: 36: 39] sts rem in chart section, 7 sts in Moss st.

NECK SHAPING

Next Row (RS): Work in Moss St and St st.
Next Row (WS): Cast off 8 [9: 10: 11: 12: 13] sts, work in patt to end. 23 [25: 27: 29: 31: 33] sts.
Next Row: Work Moss st, k2tog, knit to end. 32 [34:36: 38: 40: 42] sts.
Next Row: Cast off 8 [9: 10: 11: 12: 13] sts, work in patt to end. 24 [25: 26: 27: 28: 29] sts.
Next Row: Work Moss st, k2tog, knit to end. 23 [24: 25: 26: 27: 28] sts.
Cast off rem Yarn B sts. 7 sts.
Work in Moss St with Yarn A for 12 [13: 15: 17: 18: 20] rows. Cast off.

LEFT FRONT

Work as for Right Front reversing all shaping.

SLEEVES (MAKE 2)

Using 7mm needles and Yarn A cast on 55 [55: 55: 64: 73: 82] sts

Work in moss stitch for 10 rows.
Change to yarn B and work 2 rows in St st.
Begin working Chart A and continue until 56 rows have been worked.
Cast off.

MAKING UP

Block all pieces to dimensions given in schematic.

With RS facing, using mattress stitch, sew shoulder seams together, matching shoulders using the removable markers as a guide. Sew cast off edges of fronts together and then pin around the back neck, making sure the seam is in the centre of the back. Sew into place.

Using mattress stitch, pin the sleeves to the body and sew into place. Then sew the side seams together.

Sew in all ends.

TASSELS

Cut out 15cm (6in) lengths of Yarn A. Using a crochet hook or latchhook, fold four lengths of Yarn A together and insert into the holes made in the second row of the work. Continue all the way round the bottom of the cardigan.

SCHEMATIC

Shows finished measurements

BACK/FRONTS

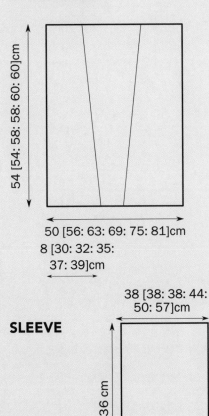

54 [54: 58: 58: 60: 60]cm

50 [56: 63: 69: 75: 81]cm

8 [30: 32: 35: 37: 39]cm

38 [38: 38: 44: 50: 57]cm

SLEEVE

36 cm

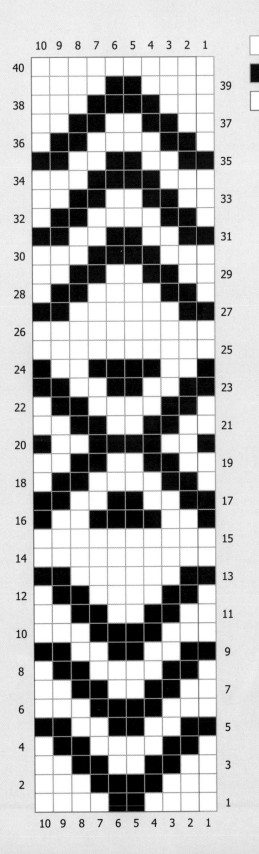

Key

White

Black

Repeat

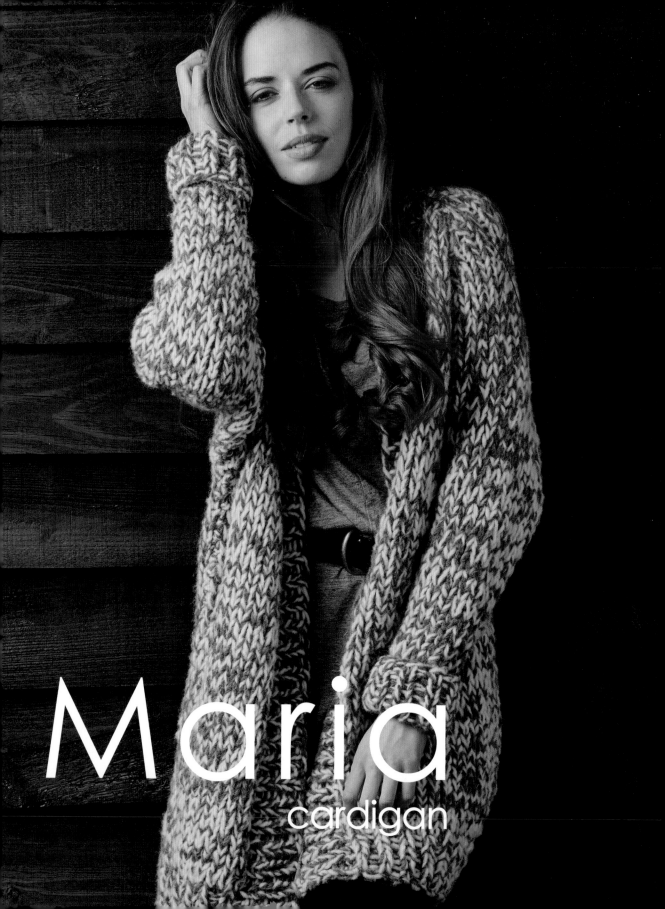

Maria
cardigan

SIZING
XS [S: M: L: XL: XXL]

Shown in size XS
See schematic for finished measurements.
For fit information, see p.80.

YARN
Rowan Brushed Fleece
A Cove 251 5 [5: 6: 6: 7: 7] x 50g
B Tarn 254 5 [5: 6: 6: 7: 7] x 50g

NEEDLES
1 pair 12mm (US 17) needles
1 pair 16mm (US 19) needles

TENSION
7 sts and 9 rows to 10cm measured over
st st using 16mm (US 19) needles and yarn
held double

OTHER SUPPLIES
Tapestry needle

PATTERN INSTRUCTIONS
BACK
Using 12mm (US 17) needles and one
strand each of A and B held together, cast
on 44 [50: 54: 58: 62: 68] sts.

Rows 1-6: *K1, P1, rep from * to end.
Change to 16mm (US 19) needles.
Row 7 (RS): Knit.
Row 8: Purl.
Rows 7-8 form st st. Cont working in st st
until work measures 45 [40: 40: 40: 38: 38]cm
from cast-on edge, ending after a WS row.

SHAPE RAGLAN
Next Row: Cast off 2 [3: 5: 6: 7: 9] sts, K to
end. 42 [47: 49: 52: 55: 59] sts.
Next Row: Cast off 2 [3: 5: 6: 7: 9] sts, P to
end. 40 [44: 44: 46: 48: 50] sts.
Next Row (dec row): K1, ssk, K to last 3
sts, k2tog, K1. 2 sts dec'd.
Next Row: Purl.
Rep these last two rows 12 [14: 14: 14: 15:
15] more times. 14 [14: 14: 16: 16: 18] sts.
Cast off.

LEFT FRONT:
Using 12mm (US 17) needles and one
strand each of A and B held together, cast
on 20 [24: 26: 28: 32: 34] sts.

Rows 1-6: *K1, P1, rep from * to end.
Change to 16mm (US 19) needles.
Row 7 (RS): Knit.
Row 8: Purl.
Rows 7-8 form st st. Cont working in st st
until work measures 45 [40: 40: 40: 38: 38]cm
from cast-on edge, ending after a
RS row.

SHAPE RAGLAN

Next Row: Cast off 2 [3: 5: 6: 7: 9] sts, P to end. 18 [21: 21: 22: 25: 25] sts.

**Next Row (raglan dec row): K1, ssk, K to end. 1 st dec'd.

Next Row: Purl.

Rep the last 2 rows 3 [2: 2: 1: 1: 1] more time(s).

Next Row (neck and raglan dec row): K1, ssk, K to last 3 sts, k2tog, K1. 2 sts dec'd.

Next Row: Purl.

Rep from ** 1 [2: 2: 3: 3: 3] more time(s).

Next Row (raglan dec row): K1, ssk, K to end. 1 st dec'd.

Next Row: Purl.

Rep these last 2 rows until 3 [3: 3: 3: 5: 5] sts rem. Cast off.

RIGHT FRONT

Work as left front reversing all shaping

SLEEVES (make 2 the same)

Using 12mm (US 17) needles and one strand each of A and B held together, cast on 18 [20: 22: 24: 26: 28] sts.

Rows 1-6: *K1, P1, rep from * to end.
Change to 16mm (US 19) needles.

Row 7 (RS): Knit.

Row 8: Purl.

Row 9: K1, M1, K to last st, M1, K1. 2 sts inc'd.

Row 10: Purl.

Rep these last 4 [4: 4: 2: 2: 2] rows 7 [9: 10: 10: 11: 12] more times.
34 [40: 44: 46: 50: 54] sts.
Cont straight until work measures 44 [45: 45: 46: 47: 48]cm, ending after a WS row.

SHAPE RAGLAN

Next Row: Cast off 2 [3: 5: 6: 7: 9] sts, K to end. 32 [37: 39: 40: 43: 45] sts.

Next Row: Cast off 2 [3: 5: 6: 7: 9] sts, P to end. 30 [34: 34: 34: 36: 36] sts.

Next Row (dec row): K1, ssk, k to last 3 sts, k2tog, k1. 2 sts dec'd.

Next Row: Purl.

Rep these last two rows 12 [14: 14: 14: 15: 15] more times. 4 [4: 4: 4: 4: 4] sts.
Cast off.

MAKING UP

Join raglans and side seams.

RIGHT FRONT EDGING

Starting at the lower edge of right front, pick up and knit 74 sts along front edge to centre back.

Rows 1-8: *K1, P1, rep from * to end.
Cast off.

LEFT FRONT EDGING

Starting at the centre of back neck and with RS facing, pick up and knit 74 sts along front edge to centre back.

Rows 1-8: *K1, P1, rep from * to end.
Cast off.
Join front edgings at centre back neck.

SCHEMATIC

Shows finished measurements

BACK/FRONTS

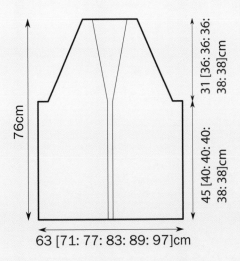

76cm

31 [36: 36: 36: 38: 38]cm

45 [40: 40: 40: 38: 38]cm

63 [71: 77: 83: 89: 97]cm

SLEEVE

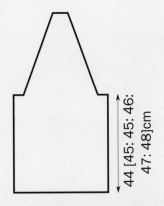

44 [45: 45: 46: 47: 48]cm

ACKNOWLEDGEMENTS

I'd like to say a big thank you to Darren and Georgie at Quail Publishing for giving me the opportunity to create this book. Jesse for his amazing photography. The Royal National Rose Garden's for letting us use their grounds and the amazing model Jeannette Belaouane for her hard work and fantastic look.

Thanks also to the Rowan team for providing the yarn for the book and the great knitter for helping bring my designs to life. Also a huge thanks to Katie for pattern checking and tech editing.

And finally thanks to all my friends and family for supporting me and putting up with my constant knitting!

Emily

ABBREVIATIONS

K – knit
P – purl
st(s) – stitch(es)
inc – increas(e)(ing)
dec – decreas(e)(ing)
st st – stocking stitch (1 row knit, 1 row purl)
g st – garter stitch (every row knit)
beg – begin(ning)
foll – following
rem – remain(ing)
alt – alternate
cont – continue
patt – pattern
tog – together
mm – millimetres
cm – centimetres
in – inch(es)
RS – right side
WS – wrong side
sl 1 – slip one stitch
psso – pass slipped stitch over
p2sso – pass 2 slipped stitches over
tbl – through back of loop
m1 – make one stitch by picking up loop between last and next stitch and working into the back of this loop
yfwd - bring yarn forward between the needles and then back over before making the next stitch. 1 st inc'd.
meas – measures
wyif – with yarn in front
wyib – with yarn at back
sm – slip marker
pm – place marker
sk2po – slip 1 stitch knitwise, knit 2 stitches together, pass slipped stitch over
dpn – double pointed needle
ssk – slip 2 stitches knitwise one at a time, knit the two slipped stitches together through the back of the loops.

SIZING FIT CHART

Woman's size	X-Small	Small	Medium	Large	1X	2X
Bust (in.)	28–30	32–34	36–38	40–42	44–46	48–50
(cm.)	*71–76*	*81–86*	*91.5–96.5*	*101.5–106.5*	*111.5–117*	*122–127*
Upper arm	9 ¾	10 ¼	11	12	13½	15½
	25	*26*	*28*	*30.5*	*34.5*	*39.5*
Armhole depth	6–6½	6½–7	7–7½	7½–8	8–8½	8½–9
	15.5–16.5	*16.5–17.5*	*17.5–19*	*19–20.5*	*20.5–21.5*	*21.5–23*
Waist	23–24	25–26 ½	28–30	32–34	36–38	40–42
	58.5–61	*63.5–67.5*	*71–76*	*81.5–86.5*	*91.5–96.5*	*101.5–106.5*
Hips	33–34	35–36	38–40	42–44	46–48	52–53
	83.5–86	*89–91.5*	*96.5–101.5*	*106.5–111.5*	*116.5–122*	*132–134.5*